Hi, Whatcha Drawing?

1 + 2

In this modern world we all scurry about busy doing our own thing. From time to time we need to remind ourselves to set time aside for things that matter: reading, writing, having coffee, going to the bathroom, or meeting with friends. It's these little moments that make life worth it.

Living is worth it. Finding happiness is worth it. Chasing your dreams is worth it.

This gigantic book you hold in your hand is a simple experiment in making your day better. I hope it makes your day better? With this simple book all you need is a pen or a pencil and your wild imagination.

This book would not exist were it not for my awesome wife who wanted things to draw. I made this book for her. She would draw stuff from my previous books, and then asked me if I had more weird scenes to challenge her artistry & imagination.

Hi, whatcha drawing?

Feel free to show them when they ask. Challenge yourself and your artistry. Get crazy. Go loco. Do whatever you want, draw whatever you want.

Sounds easy right?

If you want to spice things up, buy an extra copy for a friend, family member, or partner. Share your creations with each other. Peer into the inner workings of those dear to you. Or maybe not, omg TMI right?

If you are feeling so bold, tweet me a photo of your art **@iamBisteh** (follow me there too if you want) and I'll share your talent with the world.

Alright, I've done introduced this book enough. Time to get your draw on!

One:

Girl Interrupts Cat Doing Yoga

Two:

Kangaroo Flying A Kite Near Power Lines

Three:

Polar Bear Luau

Four:

Escher Sketch

Five:

Vengeful Raincloud vs a Bunny

Six:

Existential Penguin

Seven:

Christmas Duck

Eight:

The Slothpocalypse

Nine:

Sentient Cheese stalking a Mouse

Ten:

Your Debut Vinyl Album Cover

Eleven:

Strange Things

Twelve:

Pineapple Enjoying A Sunset

Thirteen:

Two Dogs Playing Chess

Fourteen:

Insomniac Sheep

Fifteen:

Ants Having A Picnic

Sixteen:

Giraffe's Playing Jump Rope

Seventeen:

Lighthouse Rocket Blast Off

Eighteen:

Comb Sitting in a Dentist Chair

Nineteen:

Your Worst Fear

Duck ducking from Geese

Twenty-One:

Daft Skunk

Armadillo at the Bowling Alley

Twenty-Three:

Sweet Marmot

Nihilist Nurse

Twenty-Five:

Truth in Advertising

Twenty-Six:

Make Belief

Twenty-Seven:

Knowledge is POWAH

Twenty-Eight:

G.O.A.T. Goat

Twenty-Nine:

Owls Eye Exam

Thirty:

47 Minute Electric Harp Solo

Cyborg Hampster 2077

Thirty-Two:

Bachata of the Flowers

Moon Crashing into San Francisco

Thirty-Four:

Pour A Drink for the Honey Bees

Thirty-Five:

Your Constipated Stapler

The Legend of Zebra

Thirty-Seven:

POV of a Moose tickling you with its Antlers

Retirement Party for a Plunger

Thirty-Nine:

LUL UR SO RNDM

Forty:

Potatoes Having a Laser Sword Fight

Forty-One:

Cow Does Walk of Shame

Forty-Two:

Meaning of Life

Cashew with a Human Allergy

Samurai Monkeys Duel by Moonlight

Shark Buying A Bigger Boat

Baby Carrot discovers Mind Control

Spider Betrays the Pig

Hipster Koala enjoying E-cig

Forty-Nine:

Camel stubbed its toe

Zombie Corgi Turns on its Owner

Squirrel Diversifying its Portfolio

T-Rex waiting in line for the Bathroom

This mosquito, your amigo, enjoying a Burrito

Fifty-Four:

Newborn Smartphone Baptism

Diabetic Doughnut testing its Blood Glucose level

Sad Killer Whale eating a Sandwich on a Park Bench

Fifty-Seven:

Sightless Cantaloupe

Atypical Millennial Jellyfish

Fifty-Nine:

Beetles crossing the Street

Sixty:

The Miming of the Lambs

Hermit Crab Real Estate Agent

Sixty-Two:

Dolphins Podcasting

Toilet Paper Roll Hanging the Right Way

You Realize You're In a Computer Simulation

Sixty-Five:

Pleasing Fungus Beetle

Holy Red Lipped Batfish

Aliens Return Home & Discover the Pets Ran Amok

Turtle, Parrot, and Ape Embark on an Epic Quest

Sixty-Nine:

Cthulhu Swimming

Seventy:

Afghan Hound Cosplays as a Sloth

Octopus Barista

Seventy-Two:

Cactus Gets a Flu Shot

Field Mouse playing catch with Dad

Seventy-Four:

Leprechaun getting Audited

That Turkey Shaped Library in Toronto

Seventy-Six:

Tasmanian Devil whispering in your Ear

The Angriest Canadian Ever

Seventy-Eight:

Balding Hedgehog tries a Comb Over

Man in the Moon is Evicted

Eighty:

Spoon regrets Eloping with The Dish

Eighty-One:

Middle Aged Turtle Accountants

Eighty-Two:

Badger Trying to Parallel Park

Humming Bird discovers Espresso

Eighty-Four:

State Installed Golden Retriever Spies on Family

Golden Retriever Hosting Televised Talent Show

A pitbull playing with its dolly

Eighty-Seven:

Quokka battling Depression

Viking Funeral for an Elephant

Eighty-Nine:

The Ducks of Hazard

Ninety:

Album cover "The Core" by The Fujis

Ninety-One:

Rabbit stealing eggs from the Market

Mushroom's first day at Magic School

Ninety-Three:

Bobcat in a tank top fights a fridge magnet

Ninety-Four

Tree gets prescription glasses & sees forest for the 1st time

Ninety-Five:

Chicken Crosswalk Guard

Ninety-Six:

Water Melon smashing a Comedian

Ninety-Seven:

The lesser known Eighth Deadly Sin

Nikola and Thomas Fistfight in Heaven

Unicorn doing roadside Community Service

One Hundred:

YOLO Diem

The End

(of Hi, Whatcha Drawing? Volume 1)

One:

Poodle Shreds Air Guitar

Comb got a visit from the tooth fairy

Spotted Hyena Tai Chi Master

Four:

Falling snowflake accepts the end is near but realizes it's a family reunion

Five:

Ferret misses the 90's grunge scene

Six:

Leprechaun playing the Ukulele

Seven:

Llama whip training at night

Eight:

Corn enjoying a tanning bed

Nine:

Dragon embarrassed about its Halitosis

Mockingbird gets a taste of its own medicine

Eleven:

Apple takes up Archery

Twelve:

Butter taking in a Parisian sunrise

Thirteen:

Anxious Lynx walking the streets of New York

80's Slasher Sheep Invades Your Dreams

Fifteen:

Fish Artificial Intelligence

Sixteen:

60's Hippy Deer Hitchhiking to California

Seventeen:

Termite discovers his house has a Beaver Infestation

Eighteen:

Octopus Figure Skating on the River

Nineteen:

Penguin Hang Gliding

Twenty:

Canadian Dystopian Society

boy and a Tiger sailing down the Mississippi on a raft

sloth trying to play the Harp with its claws

Wiener Dog offers ride sharing service for hamsters

Twenty-Four

Doughnut and a Bagel fistfight in Heaven

Tonsil enjoying a game of outdoor hockey with friends

Twenty-Six:

Lemur trying to play basketball vs a Giraffe

Obese cat in rehab recovering from pasta addiction

Tiger sailing down the Mississippi on a raft by itself with regrets

Mosquitofish buzzing around your ear at night

Thirty:

Mayfly Day Trader

Groundhog archaeologist in search of fortune and glory

Ladybug delivering a rousing speech to the Resistance

Husky pup realizing it might be a god of Thunder reincarnated

Thirty-Four:

Vampire discovers Blood Oranges are a lie

Thirty-Five:

Raccoon maintaining its Bonsai Tree

Thirty-Six:

Your Epiphany Face

Middle Aged Turtle Accountant Using the Paper Shredder

Thirty-Eight

Waifu Pillow becomes a legal Citizen

Thirty-Nine:

Hungover Church Bell on a Sunday Morning

Forty:

Cthulhu running a hotdog stand

Forty-One:

Firefighter riding a Dragon

Police Officer arresting a Doughnut

The One Crazy Person You Know Who Likes Comic Sans

Forty-Four:

Bald Eagle shopping for a Wig

Trumpet trying to blow up birthday Balloons

Forty-Six:

Snail with Reverse Vertigo

Forty-Seven:

California Leaf-Nose Bat Ski Jumping

Forty-Eight:

Squirrel running a Ponzi Scheme

Forty-Nine

Mongoose pretending to know how to use a game controller

Fifty:

Service-Velociraptor assisting its companion

Spider surfing the web

Fifty-Two:

Peacock takes a selfie

Fifty-Three:

Goat driving a 4x4 SUV up a Mountain

Canadian Beavers building a Wall along the US Border

Fifty-Five:

Honey bee watering its garden

Fifty-Six:

Shepherd dog hosting Pirate Radio Show

Fifty-Seven:

Pangolin leads medieval army into battle

Butterfly waiting for you at the airport holding a sign

a Peach mooning a passing Semi-truck

Sixty:

French Horn shopping for Baguettes

The Happiest Koala Ever Riding in a Kangaroo's Pouch

Sixty-Two:

Genius Goldfish Visualizing the Theory of Special Relativity

Sixty-Three:

Genius Goldfish realizes it's a goldfish

Onion with a papercut starts crying

Sixty-Five:

Pterodactyl vs a jet fighter

Sixty-Six:

Parrot recording an Audiobook

Rooster and an Alarm Clock showdown at High Noon

Dalmatian Sailing in a Hot Air Balloon

Wiener hiding in a bathtub with a paintball gun

Seventy:

Hyena Librarian tells you to Shsss

Sable throwing stuff away after reading book on Minimalism

Sable takes up Origami to replace lost possessions

Seventy-Three:

Iberian Lynx styling its mutton chops

Saturn fills up the St. Louis night sky

Axolotl auditioning for a commercial

Cow Defiantly Stares Down Approaching Tornado

Nervous birthday cake looking up at burning candles

Skeleton walking down the sidewalk holding a can of paint

Content cat sailing in its Dinghy to the Edge of the World

Eighty:

House Fly tries VR for the first time

Eighty-One:

Wolf and a Sheep trying the trust fall exercise

Radio watching your high definition TV while you're away

Policeman playing a guitar in the middle of a hockey riot

Aging vinyl album stares at the lines on his face

Moon howling at the wolves on Earth

Otter shaking its head: no

Eighty-Seven:

Quokka laying on a therapists couch

Fridge Magnet listening to a lecture about Determinism

Calico kitten receives a knitted sweater for Christmas

Ninety:

Calico kitten lying next to a bundle of yarn

Ninety-One:

Beagle sniffing deodorant

Ninety-Two:

The Sun driving an ice cream truck

Two printers making a stack of Flowers

Bee Hummingbird, Verdin, and a Gold Crest working at crisis support call center

Dog watching sad commercial about adopting human orphans

Wolf flying a helicopter

Ninety-Seven:

Boulder happily sliding down the mountain

Ninety-Eight:

Prairie dog admiring its piles of dirt

Mayfly encases itself in Amber

One Hundred:

Squirrels board their Acorn spaceship to go back Home

The End

(of Hi, Whatcha Drawing? 1 +2)

Thank you for buying this book. I hope you enjoyed it!

Hey wait, that's it? That can't be it.

I don't know if I could get away with making this book any bigger. It's a decent size blunt instrument of pain already.

If you want more books like this tweet me **@iamBisteh**

If you liked the book you're welcome to leave an honest review online.

In a previous life I wrote other books you may or may not be interested in:

"Feast: A Gitksan Story" is a story of healing after loss in northern British Columbia. An exploration of First Nations (Native American) grieving customs in this contemporary age. If you want to learn the Gitksan way of saying goodbye this is the book to read.

"Known Shippable, Will Not Fix" is a sci-fi comedy based on my life in game development. Inspired from the years I spent at Visual Concepts making the assorted 2K Sports games (basketball, baseball, hockey, and football) and my time at 2K Marin when we made BioShock 1 & 2. Known Shippable is the story of a young QA tester who discovers the world is a simulation. It's up to him to save it one bug entry at a time. A goofy comedy filled with lots of crazy nonsense.

Thank you for drawing some crazy stuff. Take care out there!

-Roy W. Russell